I'm Sorry You Were In When I Called

I'm Sorry You Were In When I Called

Conservative Anecdotes from the 1992 General Election & Others

collected by

The Rt Hon Sir John Cope MP

Foreword by

The Rt Hon Sir Norman Fowler MP

Drawings by

Philip Spence

Colt Books Ltd
Cambridge
in association with
Conservative Central Office

Colt Books Ltd
9 Clarendon Road
Cambridge CB2 2BH

in association with

Conservative Central Office,
32 Smith Square,
London SW1P 3HH

First published 1992

Text copyright © Conservative Central Office 1992
Illustrations copyright © Colt Books Ltd 1992

ISBN 0 905899 07 5

Cover illustration by Philip Spence
Cover design by Clare Byatt

British Library Cataloguing-in-Publication Data
A catalogue record for this book is available from the British Library

Printed and bound in Great Britain by Redwood Press

Contents

Foreword

General Elections are the time when politicians and the public get the clearest and closest look at each other – and it is not surprising that the results should often be humorous.

I learned that lesson in my first election campaign in Nottingham South. One of my woman canvassers knocked on a door in the constituency – and was greeted by a completely naked man. He was clearly unabashed – but Conservatives in Nottingham are used to challenges. The canvasser did not bat an eyelid – and proceeded calmly to explain that the Conservative candidate, Norman Fowler, was in the area. She asked the man whether he would like to be introduced. Suddenly his bravado vanished, and he squirmed, "I couldn't possibly meet him like this," before retreating into his house to get dressed.

I have one other enduring memory of that 1970 election campaign. The polls and pundits told us that the Conservatives would lose – but it was clear from the reaction of (clothed) people I met on the doorstep that we were going to win, which we did.

The parallel with the 1992 election campaign is obvious. It was something that the Prime Minister and I tried to point out to the pundits at the time – not that we were thanked for it either then or since!

During March and April I accompanied John Major in his tours round the country on his Battlebus. His campaign will be long remembered. The battered soapbox has already become a symbol of the Conservative cause every bit as recognised as our traditional torch of freedom.

During our visit to new offices in Birmingham, we arranged a photo-opportunity that lacked for nothing except photographers. While the Prime Minister was in the midst of the most photogenic part of his visit, the police decided that his progress should be unimpeded – and therefore herded the entire press corps into a building and locked them into it. The representatives of the media understandably wondered what had befallen them. There was much banging on the windows and ever more insistent demands to be let out. Not all was lost, however. One imprisoned photographer, balancing on someone else's shoulders, managed to get a shot of the Prime Minister through a top window. It was, he later said, his best photo of the campaign. So much for advance planning.

I warmly recommend this book, which brings together many hilarious moments from an historic campaign. It will bring many a laugh and jog many a memory. It proves once again that politics has a funny side – and an entirely unpredictable side too.

The Rt Hon Sir Norman Fowler MP
Chairman of the Conservative Party

Introduction

When the Conservative Party last year launched our earlier collection of anecdotes, *A Funny Thing Happened . . .* , we were delighted (but not, of course, surprised) by its success. Not only was it the best-selling book at the 1991 Party Conference, it was also widely distributed through national booksellers. As a result, I now come across the book in spare bedrooms and lavatories all over the country.

This has not pleased everybody. One MP, sending in an anecdote for this edition, wrote:

> "I would like to register a complaint, which is that this book has detained me in various loos for such long periods of time that the owners of the house where I happen to have been have felt obliged to check to see whether I was all right!"

I am very grateful to colleagues who have contributed their anecdotes and entirely sympathetic with one who wrote:

> "I found the whole election campaign a complete nightmare and I cannot remember a single funny incident."

Julian Critchley understandably replied:

> "I am afraid I can't really help you – I need all the jokes I can get!"

Once again, I am grateful to Martin Graham, the Conservative Research Department and Colt Books Ltd for bringing this heavyweight political project to fruition.

For my part, I have added to the normal "I'm sorry you were out when I called" card that we politicians put through people's letterboxes when they don't answer the door. I have designed a new card to give the voter who keeps you on the doorstep discussing every abstruse aspect of national and local affairs – usually just as you are supposed to be leaving that street. It reads: "I'm Sorry You Were In When I Called."

The following may help you to understand why.

The Rt Hon Sir John Cope MP
Paymaster General

I'm Sorry You Were In When I Called

Lady Olga Maitland MP

Member for Sutton and Cheam

My husband was out canvassing one evening. The door of one house opened and a very fierce woman stood there with her arms folded across her chest. After my husband finished his "spiel", he then had to listen to a litany of her complaints ending with, "What's more, I can't stand that Olga Maitland!"

My husband patiently said, "Have you ever met her?"

She replied, "No, but I hate everything I have read about her!" She then paused, looked directly at my husband and said, "What do you know about her anyway?"

My husband said, "As a matter of fact I have been married to her for twenty years."

Unabashed she said, "Rather you than me!"

Henry Bellingham MP

Member for Norfolk North West

My most memorable, but least distinguished, General Election exchange involved a visit to a flat in King's Lynn.

I was greeted at the door by a young man in his thirties, and after four or five minutes of trying to persuade him to vote for me I realised I was getting absolutely nowhere. I then heard some clattering from the room next door, and out came a fairly elderly woman, well in excess of seventy-five. After an even more unsatisfactory conversation with her, I decided it was time to cut my losses and leave. By this time the elderly lady had gone back into her bedroom, leaving her door ajar. In bidding my farewell to the young man I said that I just had to say a very quick goodbye to his mother.

All hell broke loose. It was not his mother but his wife! He started chasing me out of the flat. Whereupon she also plunged out of her bedroom to help evict me and swore that they had never been so badly insulted in their lives.

Andrew Zsigmond
Parliamentary Candidate for Liverpool Riverside, 1992

One terribly rainy afternoon, when I knocked on a door, a very nice chap said, "You could do with a cup of tea. Do you want one?" He was absolutely right, so I accepted. When we were sitting in his back kitchen he asked if I would mind if his monkey joined us for a cuppa. Thinking that this was his endearing name for his spouse I said, "I'd be delighted." He opened the door to the next room whence a fair-sized monkey ran into the kitchen, picked up a cup and started to drink the tea.

Peter Temple-Morris MP
Member for Leominster

C anvassing an 800 square mile rural constituency at least offers variety. Around 6 pm I chanced upon a lonely dwelling. I knocked. Strange sounds emanated. That awful moment arrived when lights come on and something advances from within as observed through mottled door glass. The door opened to reveal a woman of wide girth and generous proportions.

I was propelled into the kitchen and around a lamb in a pen which was bringing forth various things including those strange sounds. Into the living room I went where sat a strange and I fear abnormal young man. I advanced to shake hands and the girth disappeared, determined to make me a cup of tea. At the moment of contact, the young man grabbed not my hand but my thumb in a vice-like grip. He proceeded to play with it and bend it in the wrong direction whilst at the same time a voice from the kitchen intruded upon this nightmare by asking me what I thought of "this Council Tax, then". Release of thumb was quite impossible and things were getting painful.

Suddenly the familiar voice of Neil Kinnock came on the six o'clock news in full majestic flood. The youth looked at the television wide-eyed and quite transfixed and my thumb was immediately released. In came the girth, apologising. "We cannot stand him," she said, gesticulating at the television. Out I manoeuvred past the proffered tea and the lamb. The Labour leader's formidable oratory may not have been enough to persuade the British people but at least one Conservative candidate was supremely grateful for it!

David Amess MP

Member for Basildon

Throughout the General Election campaign I had the media circus with me. One afternoon, I had a reporter from *The Times* following myself and a group of canvassers around the constituency. I knocked on one door and a young girl answered and said, "Ooh – come and look everybody – it's David Amess." The door was flung open and there were a number of mums with their children. I hardly thought it was possible to have so many in one house. "Oh it's lovely to see ya'. Have you got a picture you could autograph?" I modestly handed one over duly signed. Just then a middle-aged man burst into the room and grabbed the card, saying, "You bleeding lot – you've never been any bleeding good over the last thirteen years!" He then tore up my picture and threw it into the air like confetti.

At this point, the young lady got hold of the man by his lapels and threw him backwards into another room. " 'Im! 'Ee's my bleeding uncle – me mother's brother," she said. " 'Ee's never been any bleeding good – you wait till I tell my mother! Anyway, Mr Amess, don't worry! We could never possibly vote Conservative, but of course we'll be voting for you in the election!"

Gordon McKelvie

Agent for Manchester Withington Conservative Association

A rather forthright lady canvassing in the Manchester Withington constituency came upon a rather large gentleman who was obviously not one of our supporters. After a short discussion his front door was slammed in her face. To everyone's surprise she proceeded to knock once again on his door. When it was opened, before the man had an opportunity to say anything, she said, "Excuse me, sir, I don't think you closed your front door properly." And with that she promptly walked away.

Tony Baldry MP

Member for Banbury, Parliamentary Under Secretary of State for the Environment

A s a Junior Planning Minister, I never now underestimate the challenges of planning decisions. I had a portent of this during the General Election campaign.

Calling at a village house, I was robustly assured that everyone in the house was Conservative. I was just about to mark my canvass card and go merrily on my way, when I was also told that not one of those living there would be able to vote for me. I asked why, anticipating that they might be eligible for a postal vote.

"It's the village hall," came the answer.

"What's wrong with the village hall?"

"It's in the wrong place."

"What do you mean, it's in the wrong place?"

"Well, when they decided to build the new village hall, half the village objected to the site that was chosen. They went and built it there regardless and we all vowed never to set foot in the village hall. The polling station is in the village hall and, as we're determined not to go into the village hall, we can't vote!"

I'm still trying to work out what sort of postal vote form to give them.

David Mitchell MP

Member for Hampshire North West
(Minister of State for Transport, 1990-91)

I was canvassing in the Army married quarters in Middle Wallop when the door was opened by an attractive young wife. I started my usual patter, "I am David Mitchell, your Conservative candidate. I am getting around meeting people because I think they like to see the man they are asked to vote for . . ." At that point a red setter dog appeared. I bent down and stroked the dog's head and said, "Aren't you beautiful, aren't you gorgeous, I would like to take you home with me." At that point the election calm was shattered by a furious husband who appeared with a clenched fist. He had apparently been standing within earshot and had not realised that I had been addressing the dog and not his wife. I fled.

Rupert Allason MP
Member for Torbay

L ate one wet evening, towards the end of the General Election campaign, I was canvassing with a team of helpers, among whom was my Association President. He directed me to one house and said, "You should be all right there."

This was the last street to be called on, and it had been raining much of the evening, so I was slightly bedraggled and my anorak was obscuring my rosette. The door was answered by a middle-aged gentleman and I proceeded to give him my usual patter. "Good evening, sir, I'm Rupert Allason, your Conservative candidate at the election next week and I do hope I can count on your support . . ." At that moment I was interrupted by a lady with a towel around her head who suddenly emerged from an inner room and angrily demanded to know why I was calling so late. "I don't think eight o'clock is particularly late," I countered, "and I have a lot of people to call on."

"But you didn't let us know you were coming," she complained.

Slightly puzzled, I told her it was impossible to let individual householders know when I proposed to call on them. There were simply too many people to see.

"That's preposterous," she insisted. "What would have happened if we had been out?"

"That's no problem," I answered easily, indicating a pile of leaflets attached to my clipboard. "I've plenty of literature to leave behind." This seemed to enrage her.

"Literature?" she exploded. "Good grief, it's too late for literature," and she stormed out of the hall, slamming an inner door. Her husband appeared embarrassed at her outburst, just as I was, and I made my retreat covered in confusion. When I rejoined my team, I told them I had just met a most unreasonable woman who apparently expected me to telephone every voter to make an appointment to canvass them. We all had a good chuckle at the ridiculous notion of making appointments.

Two nights later I received quite a surprise. While canvassing at the opposite end of the constituency I called at a house on a large modern estate. The woman who answered the door looked embarrassed when I introduced myself.

"You called on my mother the night before last, and she was dreadfully rude to you," she said. Somewhat sheepishly I confirmed that I had not forgotten the incident.

"She had been waiting in all day for the man to repair her new conservatory but he had never turned up. When she heard you mention the Conservatives she thought you were the builder. Far from being sorry for the inconvenience and the lateness of your call, you seemed quite unapologetic and then, to add insult to injury, you apparently said you would have left some more of the wretched conservatory brochures if she had been out. She was hopping mad . . . until my father explained to her later who you really were."

Michael Bates MP

Member for Langbaurgh

Whilst canvassing in Skelton at the height of the debate over "Jennifer's ear" I called at a house where I was greeted warmly by the constituent who said, "It's about time we had a decent candidate around these parts." I was pleased to receive this popular affirmation in what was for us not one of our best areas. He then went on to say, "How right you are to stay out of this whole debate about Jennifer's ear. The Labour Party and the Conservative Party are always at each others throats and I think that your leader is so right to stay out of the whole thing."

Wondering if I had in some way misled him, I pointed out that I was the Conservative Party Candidate. I was after all, wearing my blue rosette. At once he offered his profuse apologies, and said that he was colour blind!

Laurence Robertson
Parliamentary Candidate for Ashfield, 1992

A group of us were canvassing together on a new estate, with a lady who was educated at Oxford and spoke with the appropriate accent – for Oxford, not for the estate. She went down a cul-de-sac on her own, only to be shouted and sworn at by a loud-mouthed person leaning out of a window.

She returned to our group and, obviously slightly rattled, began telling us the tale. We started to feel sorry for her until she said in perfect English: "But at least I had the presence of mind to lower my voice before I told him to **** Off!"

David Amess MP

Member for Basildon

One evening I was campaigning in Pitsea. I knocked on a door and a young woman opened it who was obviously pleased to see me. She called back into the house, "Look, it's David Amess!" A girl called back, "Oh I know all about 'im. 'Ee supports Margaret Thatcher and she's Rank Labour!"

Irvine Patnick MP

Member for Sheffield Hallam, Lord Commissioner of the Treasury

During municipal elections some years ago when I was a Councillor, I was door-to-door canvassing when a man said that he would vote for me if I could answer a question. "Is it true that Councillors do not have to pay rates?" I explained that this was not so, and that Councillors had to pay like anybody else. The man replied, "If tha can do nowt for theesen, tha' can do nowt for me."

Michael Trend MP

Member for Windsor and Maidenhead

Canvassing during the 1992 General Election, I came across a man who was positively not going to vote Conservative because of the way we had treated our

Leader. I expressed my regret at this and said that of course Margaret Thatcher was a great Leader and had done much for the nation but . . .

"It's not Margaret Thatcher I'm talking about you fool," said the irate voter, "I'm talking about Ted Heath."

Hugh Dykes MP

Member for Harrow East

When canvassing on the doorstep, with everyone in a bad mood because of the weather, Hugh Dykes came face to face with a reluctant voter:

Voter: All right, I will vote for you this time but I am not too keen on Europe, you know. In fact, I don't think we should join the Community at all.

Mr Dykes: (totally astonished) But . . . we joined in 1973!

Voter: (looking pitying and scornful) No, no, dear boy, get your facts right. That was the Commonwealth.

The Clincher

Sir John Lacy

(General Director of Party Campaigning, Conservative Central Office 1988-92)

During the General Election campaign I was delighted to receive three tips from one of my colleagues, David Roberts, at that time, the Central Office Agent in the Northern Area.

Tip One: Party Politics to win the Grand National at Aintree on 4 April

Tip Two: Oxford to win the Boat Race on 4 April

Tip Three: John Major to win the General Election on 9 April

My comment was: "Well done, David – a nice treble – thank you!"

Jim Lester MP

Member for Broxtowe, Under Secretary of State for Employment

I had hastily grabbed a handful of our short manifesto pamphlets from a box that had arrived from Central Office, before going out to meet people in Beeston Town

Square during the General Election campaign. So, when one of my constituents raised questions on immigration in a rather voluble manner, I offered him a copy of the manifesto pamphlet to take away and read.

Too late, one of my helpers said, "Do you realise what you have given him?" I had handed out a copy printed entirely in Urdu and other foreign languages.

I reckon I probably lost his vote!

Martin Winter

Parliamentary Candidate for Tooting, 1992

I broke my ankle before the election but despite being cased in plaster and walking with two crutches there was no real difficulty in getting to the top of any block of flats. I generally received credit for doing so.

On one occasion a cross-sounding lady grudgingly let me in via her entryphone, saying, "I can't come down, you know." When I got to her flat at the top of a particularly long staircase I found her crossness had turned to laughter – she had a much smaller plaster and a single crutch.

Whether she voted for me, who knows, but she certainly promised she would.

Stuart Sexton
Parliamentary Candidate for Workington, 1992

G ood humoured hectoring at a bustling public meeting is almost a thing of the past, as so many people stay indoors in front of the television. Nevertheless, I had high hopes for our public meeting in Keswick. A well-known, vociferous Labour councillor met me on the steps of the Moot Hall as I arrived for the meeting. We should have a lively meeting after all, I thought.

"Coming in?" I said brightly.

"No," he replied, "I just came to apologise that I won't be attending your meeting. It's the last showing tonight of the film JFK."

I wonder. Had he got his priorities right?

Nigel Evans MP
Member for Ribble Valley

N igel Evans, a Welshman, who fought the Ribble Valley by-election was the victim of attacks throughout the period of the by-election about the fact that he was not a Lancastrian; indeed, he had come from Wales. At the following General Election he again contested the Ribble Valley seat.

While he was standing outside a polling station, a gentleman came up to him, shook him warmly by the hand and said, "I'm voting for you. We don't want that Welsh git Kinnock in power do we?"

Mr Evans smiled sweetly and replied, "No we don't."

The result was that the "Welsh git" didn't get to No 10 and Mr Evans became Member of Parliament for the Ribble Valley.

Greg Knight MP

Member for Derby North, Lord Commissioner of the Treasury

J ust before the 1992 election, I was asked to open a charity event in aid of animal welfare. After my opening remarks, I walked around the stalls to meet those who were helping with the fundraising. I was approached by a little old lady who said she was "delighted" to meet me and she thanked me for all of the good work I had done over the years. I naturally accepted her thanks and assured her that I would continue to do whatever I could for the area. She then went on to say how much pleasure and happiness I had brought into her life and the lives of many others, adding, "You really are a wonderful, wonderful person."

Thinking this praise was slightly over the top, I nevertheless continued to humour her and told her that I had only done what I regarded to be my duty. As I was about to depart she grabbed my arm and told me that life would be much duller for thousands of local people if I was ever to leave. "I hear you on the radio and you're really good," she continued.

I modestly thanked her again and added that I had not actually been on the radio for a couple of weeks, at which point she raised her voice and said, "Don't give me that. I heard you on the radio this morning. I listen to your show every day."

I realised by now she thought I was Graham Knight, one of the presenters on our local radio station. But not wishing to miss the opportunity, I said to her, "Well don't forget to vote for me on April 9th."

Graham Robb

Parliamentary Candidate for Hartlepool, 1992

I attended a meeting of the Christian Election Forum. The Labour candidate refused to come, but some of his supporters turned up to heckle. One of them was clearly drunk. I won the audience over by telling him: "Stand by that wall, sir – that's plastered too."

Harry Greenway MP

Member for Ealing North

The following is a true story. It occured in the Hobbayne Ward of the Ealing North Constituency during the 1992 Election.

Canvasser to an elector in Hanwell: "I am calling on behalf of Harry Greenway, our MP for the past thirteen years and Prospective Conservative Parliamentary Candidate for the General Election of April 9th. Do you think that you would be able to support Mr Greenway with your vote on April 9th?"

Lady elector: "I have to tell you that I have never voted Conservative in my life. However, have you seen the curtains at the Kinnock house in South Ealing?"

Canvasser: "No."

Lady elector: "They are absolutely filthy and I will never vote Labour again. I am voting for Mr Greenway this time and I shall always vote Conservative in the future!"

Sir Teddy Taylor MP

Member for Southend East

With my rather unofficial views I thought I was on a real winner when I was cross-examined by an elderly constituent in Shoeburyness. He said his vote would depend on my answer to four questions.

"Are you against the European Community?" he asked. I confirmed that I had spent my parliamentary life fighting this grotesque and socialist protection racket.

"Do you support hanging?" Of course I do and the records show my votes on each occasion, I was able to assure him.

"Are you opposed to fox hunting?" he asked in a challenging way. Yes, I was glad to tell him that I voted against fox hunting in the recent vote.

He finally asked if I regarded the CAP as a huge waste of money. My positive answer with a smile was, I thought, the final reassurance.

However, this difficult and challenging voter then stepped back and said, "Your replies are very reassuring, but I am not prepared to vote for someone who has not polished his shoes." Before I could reply the door closed and that was that.

Elizabeth Holt

Parliamentary Candidate for The Wrekin, 1992

People have strange reasons for voting in a particular way. During the election campaign the local paper sent a questionnaire to all the candidates asking us our various likes and dislikes. This was light relief from all the more serious surveys and filling it in caused much hilarity.

My favourite foods are black pudding and banana sandwiches. I had a furious message from a vegetarian who said she could never vote for someone who liked black pudding – but on the other hand the banana sandwiches were a great bonus, much mentioned while out and about in the constituency. One voter even summoned me to her house. Thinking the enquiry related to an urgent local problem I arrived promptly on her doorstep to be greeted with a huge plate of banana sandwiches and effusive pledges of support. "We never bothered to vote before, but we'll vote for banana sandwiches."

Records showed that they did all vote. I only hope their tastes didn't change in the intervening days.

Anthony Henfrey

Parliamentary Candidate for Berwick upon Tweed, 1992

During a canvass in Berwick upon Tweed I stopped a man in the market and asked him how he intended voting. "For you," he replied decisively. When asked why, his reply was, "I always vote for the woman on the ballot paper and if there is no woman then I vote for the youngest candidate." With me being the youngest (at 47!) of the three male candidates I got his vote.

His logic was impeccable!

Roy Thomason MP

Member for Bromsgrove

A constituent on whom I called one Saturday evening advised me that she was a floating voter. I pressed her as to the identity of the party for whom she had previously voted to see if there was any hope of persuading her to our cause. She thought for a moment or two and said that she seemed to think that she had voted for the Green Party last time.

As I started backing away I asked her if there were any particular issues of concern to her and she told me that there were not but she would definitely be voting. "I always vote," she said. "What I do is to go down to the polling station, get the ballot paper, go into the polling booth, close my eyes and put my finger on the ballot paper. I then vote for the person where my finger rests. You never know, you might get my vote after all!" she added.

I left thinking what a funny thing democracy is.

James Pawsey MP

Member for Rugby and Kenilworth

D uring the General Election we always had a very large and strong "Candidate's Team." Each night it would descend upon a given area and undertake a detailed canvass. Our opponents were at a loss as to why there was so much competition to become a member of this large but exclusive group.

At the end of a canvass, we would draw up in a side road of the estate we had been covering and then, despite the teeming rain and the steamy interior of the Battlebus, out it would come. It was amazing how it lightened and cheered the atmosphere! The secret was a large bottle of Scotch kept in the glove compartment – which every night was magically replenished.

Tony Baldry MP

Member for Banbury, Parliamentary Under Secretary of State for the Environment

One afternoon in a village on the outskirts of Banbury, I heard one of my canvassing team ask a lady if she would vote for me. The answer was an emphatic NO!

The canvasser, somewhat bravely, asked, "Oh, why is that?"

"It's the teeth."

"The teeth?"

"Yes, I can't stand any more of that bright, cheery smile peering up at me week after week from the Banbury Guardian."

I have many liabilities, but hitherto I had never thought of my teeth as being one of them.

From now on, I shall disguise my naturally sunny disposition with the occasional scowl for the benefit of those who don't like to see me happy. And I shall never underestimate the number of reasons why people don't vote for me.

Anthony Nelson MP

Member for Chichester, Economic Secretary to the Treasury

The depth and severity of the recession in the residential property market came home to me when I was canvassing in Selsey, normally a staunchly Conservative village near Chichester. I met a lady who appeared to be a likely supporter and said, "You look like a True Blue, can I count on your support at the Election?"

"Oh yes," she said, "I have seen your blue posters outside so many houses locally. This time I am definitely voting Nationwide!"

Lance Anisfield

Former Special Adviser to Peter Lilley

The Conservative 1992 Election Manifesto ended on an inspiring note – about making a dream a reality and achieving "the very best future for Britain".

The Labour Party's 1992 Election Manifesto ended on an equally appropriate note – wet fish in the Antarctic!

If you don't believe it, you can check and see for yourself.

Glyn Môn Hughes

Parliamentary Candidate for Birkenhead, 1992

My greatest campaign boost came at the start of the General Election Campaign when, due to an error in colour printing, *The Sunday Times* showed Birkenhead as a safe Tory seat, unlikely to change hands.

During the campaign, a number of young people worked with me and we plastered a red (the only colour we could get – honestly!) 35cwt van with posters, streamers, balloons and the loudest tannoy you've ever heard. We drove to the busy market and shopping centre and were promptly assailed by an extremely scruffy young gentleman who had a pit bull terrier in tow. He had something of a tantrum by our van, to the obvious delight of passers-by, accusing the Tories of preventing him getting a job. I chickened out of confronting him, on account of the dog, you must understand. So he must have been all the more surprised to hear, "You'd get a job if you got your hair cut," come booming out at 120 decibels. Fortunately for us, the van was a fast mover.

Beyond the Call of Duty

Robin Hodgson

Chairman, West Midlands Conservative Council

It is the evening of Election Day and only an hour or two before the close of the poll. The candidate in a critical marginal seat is desperately going from door to door seeking the last few supporters who have not been to vote. He goes up the steps to a rather grimy house and knocks at the door. There is a long pause. Just as the candidate is about to leave, believing the house to be empty, a shuffling is heard inside. The door swings open to reveal an incredibly ancient lady bent over her stick. The candidate explains that according to the canvass records she is a Conservative supporter and is marked as not yet having voted. After a further long pause, during which the candidate wonders if the ancient lady has understood what he has been saying, she finally looks him in the eye and asks him to wait. Off she shuffles very slowly. There is a further long pause and again the candidate wonders if she has completely forgotten about his existence. Eventually he hears a further shuffling and the ancient lady reappears, looks round the door and says to him, "Mother says we have been."

The Rt Hon Norman Lamont MP

Member for Kingston upon Thames, Chancellor of the Exchequer

In the days before television, when Conservative candidates were men of substantial means, they would address several village meetings on every night of an election campaign. One such Knight of the Shires, tiring in his task, asked his chauffeur to assume his identity, and to address one such meeting in the tiniest and most remote village hall. "You know the speech off by heart," he said to his trusty driver. "I'll doze at the back of the hall."

The meeting went well and the speech was greeted with applause. At question time, the chauffeur was fluent, until he was asked a particularly complex question about the gold standard. He contemplated the question.

"That's a very simple question to answer," he replied positively. "So simple in fact, I'm going to ask my chauffeur, who is seated at the back of the hall, to answer it!"

Michael Stephen MP

Member for Shoreham, West Sussex

While we were driving past a house in our Battlebus a man stood at the garden gate giving us the thumbs down. He must have wondered why we were smiling. His wife was at the front door behind him giving us the thumbs up!

Malcolm Thornton MP

Member for Crosby

Whilst canvassing during the early part of the campaign – when the opinion polls were causing flutters – I knocked on a door in Formby. An elderly couple came to the door, greeted me by name (always a pleasant surprise) and responded to my query as to their voting intentions by vehemently stating, "We are not just *voting* for you, we are *praying* for you!"

With a more than doubled majority, I think their prayers worked!

Stuart Sexton

Parliamentary Candidate for Workington, 1992

In the 1979 Election I was PA to Mark Carlisle, now Lord Carlisle, who was fighting the Runcorn constituency. A group of us were canvassing a housing estate.

"Leave that one to Stuart," requested Mark.

"Why so, what's special about that household?" I asked.

"You'll see."

I did. The lady of the house opened the door, completely starkers!

Ted Gale

Agent for Havant Conservative Association

In the run up to the General Election Councillor Ted Gale, Vice Chairman of Hayling Branch, read in the local "freebie" that a resident with obvious Labour sympathies was aghast when recently moving to Hayling to find there was no Labour Party Branch. Having established the lady's identity and address, Ted Gale, with some trepidation approached her door armed with John Major's publication _Transforming Britain_ and a Conservative membership book.

A somewhat frail lady in her eighties came to the door and welcomed him in, believing him initially to be a Labour Party supporter who wished to make contact, and there being no Alsation dog or other unfriendly residents in the house, Ted Gale quietly gained confidence, particularly when the whisky bottle appeared. During the drinking session that followed he eventually admitted his true identity, which was accepted with good grace.

Needless to say he did not join up the lady, but left her with _Transforming Britain_ and in return he received a copy of Dennis Healey's memoirs.

Julia Kernick

Agent and Secretary for Ealing Acton Conservative Association

We had a call from a gentleman who said he was over eighty, he had always voted Conservative and used to live in our constituency but had now moved and would like to come back to vote in Ealing Acton if we could provide transport. When asked where he now lived, he named a small village near Southampton.

Stephen Milligan MP

Member for Eastleigh

When I was visiting the polling stations on Election Day, I encountered a Liberal Democrat teller. She apologised to me for the fact that her husband had been rude to me during the election and then added confidentially: "Mr Milligan, I work for the Liberal Democrats. But I always vote Conservative."

Martin Graham

Deputy Director, Conservative Research Department

Labour's attacks took on many forms. In the run-up to the Election, one of the Party Chairman's secretaries at Central Office, Caroline Warburton, innocently went out to buy a plant. Unfortunately, the one she came back with died within the week. Or perhaps we should say fortunately. Here's why.

Not many days after returning the plant to the shop, there was a knock on her door. It turned out to be a policeman, accompanied by a pest control officer. Rather brusquely, they instructed her – with no explanation – to vacate her flat and close all the windows.

Only later did it emerge what had happened. The shop had sent the dead plant to the laboratory, for investigation. The lab found, nestling in the plant pot, a nest of baby tarantulas. The problem (if this were not problem enough) was that there was no mother tarantula to be found. The police were duly sent to investigate the flat – that of our dear Caroline – where the plant had last resided.

I'm afraid it doesn't make the story any more palatable to disclose that the pest control officer did indeed find the mother – under Caroline's mattress! Tough business, politics.

David Madel MP

Member for Bedfordshire South West

I was canvassing in a good area in my constituency and one of my supporters had his five-year-old son with him, who was making himself very useful opening and closing gates for us. His father had had a very successful afternoon, with many positive replies, until finally he knocked on a door which was opened by a very large man, who said in no uncertain terms that he would not vote Conservative. The little boy looked him carefully up and down, and then said in tones of complete amazement: "But why not?"

Andrew Saywood

Glanford and Scunthorpe Conservative Association

One cold, damp evening whilst canvassing in Scunthorpe during the 1992 General Election, a party worker knocked upon the door of a house to be confronted by two burglars. They were busily stacking the occupant's electrical equipment inside the french windows before making their getaway. Unwilling to give their voting intentions to the canvasser, the burglars took flight.

The home owner had been asleep upstairs and, not surprisingly, was terribly distressed by this, but was comforted by our party worker. Meanwhile, the chairman, Gerald Denton, set off in his jeep in hot pursuit after the burglars, followed by Sir Reginald Sheffield in his estate car and myself in our campaign vehicle.

The criminals made a clean getaway – which is probably just as well as Gerald was going to lock them in the "dog box" of his jeep overnight!

Peter Morton

Acting Agent for Portsmouth South Conservative Association

T owards the end of the campaign the only parts of the constituency still to be canvassed were the worst council blocks where we have very little support. At about tea time a lady 'mutual aider' dressed in black whom we had not seen before, turned up unexpectedly at the Campaign Office. She was alone and it was explained to her that we were canvassing the council blocks and that she really ought to wait for someone else to accompany her. "Don't worry about that," she said "I'll be all right."

By eight o'clock all the other canvassers had returned, and at nine, when it was quite dark they were beginning to get quite worried in the Campaign Office. Opinion was divided as to whether she had just gone home without bothering to return her canvass cards or whether she was in trouble. A search for her was regarded as a needle in a haystack enterprise and the Agent was just about to telephone the police when she walked in.

"Sorry I'm a bit late," she said. "I haven't quite finished what you gave me, and it was so interesting that I quite lost track of the time."

The Rt Hon Sir Edward Heath MP

Member for Old Bexley and Sidcup
(Prime Minister 1970-74)

I was delighted to be invited by Chris Patten to campaign with him once again in Bath, an hour's drive away from my home in Salisbury. I have always had the greatest

44

admiration for Chris ever since I got to know him in the Conservative Research Department when I was leader of the Party.

On the chosen midweek afternoon Chris was kept at Central Office with the repercussions of Labour's Party Political Broadcast on "Jennifer's ear", but his delightful wife accompanied me when we weighed into the crowds flooding the Bath streets.

Then the problem hit us. Everyone we encountered was only too pleased to stop and shake hands, or even have an exchange of views. But how were we to get the votes for Chris?

The first couple we encountered said yes, they would vote Conservative and would be home in Sheffield in time to do so. The next pair rushed up to me saying that they come from my home town of Broadstairs and did not expect to see me in Bath. What message could they take back for polling day?

A rather boisterous group looked somewhat surprised at being introduced to me, said it was an interesting experience and quite different from their usual election campaign in Philadelphia, USA. They introduced friends from their own group tour from Cincinatti, Chicago, San Francisco and Oregon, all of whom denied that they voted in Bath.

But then we got nearer home. Supporters from Southampton and Bournemouth, Bristol and Gloucester emerged. Meanwhile we were looking frantically for a voter from Bath.

Our search was overtaken by a very large group of mostly young people who proclaimed that they represented Paris. And liked Bath. As did a couple who confessed they were on a shopping expedition from Cardiff.

Being somewhat internationally minded myself this was thrilling stuff. But, unlike the Essex man, the Bath man appeared to have disappeared. Where were they all?

The day was saved by an elderly couple who when challenged agreed that they were Bath voters but also admitted that they were about to go on holiday to Majorca. But all was well – they had a postal vote which they had used for Chris Patten.

Julia Kernick
Agent and Secretary for Ealing Acton Conservative Association

There were several surprised faces in Ealing Broadway late in the afternoon of polling day on hearing the voice emanating from the microphone in the Conservative campaign vehicle. The voice belonged to Dmitri, a 23-year old Russian from Moscow. His message: "I come from Russia. Socialism destroyed my country. Don't let it destroy yours. Vote Conservative, vote for Sir George Young."

Needless to say he received numerous calls of support from the bystanders.

Nick Hawkins MP
Member for Blackpool South

On election night, after celebrating the narrow victories in Blackpool South and North, which defied Labour and the pundits, my wife and I returned to our home in the constituency about 5 am. On reaching our front door we turned to each other and said, "Who's got the key?"

Of the three sets of door keys, one set had been given to my parents-in-law, who were inside fast asleep, having been looking after our three children during the day. My wife had given her set to my brother who, after campaigning for us had been unsure whether he was going to stay the night or return home. We told him that if he decided to go home to post the keys through the door – and we could see them lying on the mat inside, out of reach. And my set had been in my overcoat pocket, and my overcoat had been left in the "Election Day car", which had been taken several miles out of Blackpool by my driver, who had intended to bring the coat back when he met us for dinner. But as he decided to use his wife's car he'd inadvertently left it behind.

So all in all, having been elected to "the House", I then couldn't get into my own!

Margaret Daly MEP
Member for Somerset and Dorset West

I joined a team of canvassers, all beautifully dressed in Julian Davidson sweatshirts. We drove into the centre of Yeovil and got out in the main shopping precinct to give out our leaflets. After 45 minutes or so, we all got back in the minibus and heard sounds of loud crying. We could not discover where this was coming from. We searched the bus but could not find a thing.

As we drove off, the crying continued and we saw people pointing to the roof of the minibus. There we found a cat belonging to the neighbour of the Yeovil Conservative office. It was very frightened. Julian climbed on the roof, rescued the poor animal and we did a detour by way of the Yeovil office before heading for our next assignment – not before one of our team took full advantage of the photo opportunity.

Barry Field MP
Member for Isle of Wight

On Polling Day I went round the committee rooms and a 95-year-old told me he had been the second person to vote at the polling station that morning. He always took the trouble in a General Election to vote as early as possible as, in view of his great age, he took the view that he couldn't be certain that he might not deprive the Party of a vote if he left it until later in the day.

I thought it was a most charming and very committed philosophy.

similarly

Dame Jill Knight MP
Member for Birmingham Edgebaston

The little lady was friendly, fluttery and elderly. I canvassed her the day before the Election. She greeted me warmly. "Don't you worry, Dame Jill," she said, "I shall be there at the polling station at 7.20 tomorow morning without fail."

I smiled thankfully and asked her if she was going out for the day, intending to say that I hoped she had a good one.

"Oh no," came the answer, "but I am 85 and you never know, I might get at heart attack at 7.30."

Malcolm Thornton MP

Member for Crosby

This anecdote must come very close to the ultimate in dedication to duty and "the cause".

My superb postal votes officer is well known for her ability to garner in every possible vote. Unfortunately, her husband suffered a heart attack two days before the last date for postal votes to be registered. She actually got him to sign a form whilst in intensive care! Happily, he is now well on the way to a full recovery.

Joan Miller

Agent for Wolverhampton South West Conservative Association

Three lady Wulfrunians were canvassing, per "Mutual Aid", in a district quite unfamiliar to them, when they became aware that a man was following them. When they continued their canvassing in the next road, he still followed.

At first they tried to ignore him. But whenever they looked round, he was still there. However, in the end they decided to turn and face him. They asked him what he was doing.

He was somewhat embarrassed, and explained that he had been following them hoping to find out which party they represented. His reason – that he wanted to join the Conservatives!

Julian Davidson

Parliamentary Candidate for Yeovil, 1992

With primary schools able to determine their own priorities under Local Management in Schools, some are electing to have animals and nature areas within schools. A local school labrador gave birth to three puppies at the start of the election campaign. A pupil called Amy was stroking these tiny puppies in the corner of the classroom when the teacher came across and said, "What are you going to call our new puppies, Amy?"

Amy thought for a moment and then said, "I'm going to call this one Paddy . . . and this one Alan . . . and this one Des."

The teacher enquired why and Amy replied, "Because they're Liberal Democrat puppies, Miss."

The teacher was a member of the local Liberal Democrats and lo and behold a visit from the candidate was arranged with a full complement of press the following week. "Come this way," said the teacher. "This shows you how far the influence of the Party has reached." Once again Amy was sitting with the puppies and the teacher asked her to tell the visitors what they were called. "This one is called John . . . this is Michael . . . and this one is Douglas," Amy said.

The teacher, annoyed, said sternly, "But you told me they were Liberal Democrat puppies."

Amy looked up and said, "Yes, Miss, but now their eyes have opened!"

The Hon Timothy Sainsbury MP

Member for Hove, Minister for Trade

"Have a First Aid Kit in the campaign wagon," suggested the Agent.

"No, no, it takes up too much space. We need lots of sharp pencils instead," the candidate, Tim Sainsbury, replied.

Campaigning started in earnest. Several hours of canvassing later the candidate returned with a blooded hankie and plaster on his finger.

Had he spilt blood defending Conservative principles? No, he had stabbed himself on one of the sharp – all too sharp – pencils!

Vivian Bendall MP

Member for Ilford

On Polling Day, 9 April 1992, I did my usual tour of all the polling stations. It was a beautiful day and I noticed that many people were enjoying the sunshine and the chance to get out, especially the disabled. One elderly constituent laboriously made his way in to vote using a zimmer frame. He greeted me warmly and assured me I would have his vote. His wife hung back a little, letting him go in independently, and muttered as she passed: "I don't know why he's bothering 'cos I'm going to vote against you."

The Gift of Language

Dame Shirley Oxenbury
Secretary to the Party Chairman

The Chairman's office received a message from one of our election-time temporary receptionists. "Large freezer here," he told us in his own inimitable accent.

Two of us went down to Reception to ask for this mysterious "large freezer," only to be greeted by Lord Fraser. Whoops!

John Butcher MP
Member for Coventry South West, Under Secretary of State for Education

Pensioner supporter seeking to encourage candidate: "Don't worry, Mr Butcher, you'll absolutely scrape it."

Graham Robb
Parliamentary Candidate for Hartlepool, 1992

I had the dubious pleasure of standing against Peter Mandelson at the Election. I knocked on the door of one old man who confirmed that he would, of course, support me, and certainly not Mendelssohn. "Who wants a composer as their MP?" he said.

Deborah Slattery

Agent for Norwich North

We were very fortunate to have an American research student with us for the campaign. I overheard the following conversation:

AMERICAN: (To heavily pregnant woman) Good morning Ma'am. I am calling on behalf of your Conservative candidate Patrick Thompson to see whether he can count on your support at the General Election next week?

LADY: Well there are one or two things that I am not sure about, I haven't made my mind up yet.

AMERICAN: Could it be true to say then Ma'am that you are leaning towards Labour?

LADY: (with a wry grin on her face and pointing to her large bump) Yes, I think you probably could say that I am.

Laurence Robertson

Parliamentary Candidate for Ashfield, 1992

A colleague was taking me round his village, introducing me to his neighbours and asking them to vote for me. At one house, the lady said she'd always voted Conservative and would be doing so on this occasion as well.

"What about your husband?" asked my friend.

"Yes, he'll vote Conservative as well. But my father can't, because he's dead at the moment."

Martin Graham

Deputy Director, Conservative Research Department

During the election campaign, Michael Hendrie, husband of Denise who worked for the Research Department, had a satellite dish installed at their house in Battersea and was there when the engineer came to fit it. Polite conversation ensued:

SATELLITE DISH FELLOW: What about this election campaign then? Who do you want to go for?

MICHAEL HENDRIE: Well my wife works for Tory Party Central Office, so I'd be shot if I didn't vote Tory!

SATELLITE DISH FELLOW: [pause] . . . Oh! . . . I don't know about *them* – I'm voting Conservative.

John Marshall MP

Member for Hendon South

In the 1964 General Election one of the issues was the future of the British nuclear deterrent. On one doorstep a constituent said that she would vote for me in order to preserve the independent detergent!

Mary Gibbon

Parliamentary Candidate for Wallsend, 1992

I was fighting the Wallsend seat. Stephen Byers was the new Labour candidate following the retirement of Ted Garret. The Labour majority was approximately 19,000.

Whilst out canvassing the following conversation took place:

"Good morning. My name is Mary Gibbon. I am the Conservative candidate and I wondered if you will be voting for me on April 9th?"

"Ee pet, you've got a tough job on your hands round here. You know if Labour put up a monkey round here it would get in."

"Well, you know my name is Gibbon. Why do you think the Conservatives selected me?"

John Marshall MP

Member for Hendon South

At an earlier election I was taking part in an open debate with my two opponents. There was a question on overseas aid and the Liberal candidate insisted on answering it first and he started by saying that what was needed was a second Marshall Plan. He was somewhat confused by the smiles across my supporters' faces and felt he had to repeat himself. When he did so a number of them shouted "Hear hear!" From then on his performance deteriorated dramatically!

The Rt Hon Peter Lilley MP

Member for St Albans, Secretary of State for Social Security

On page 18 of the Labour Party's 1992 Election Manifesto, a lengthy paragraph about education was followed by a very similar lengthy paragraph about education. In fact – to be frank – it was a word-for-word repeat, all ten lines of it.

This revealing mess-up came under the heading: "Guaranteed Standards".

Sir Peter Tapsell MP
Member for Lindsey East

My wife is French. She speaks fluent English but with a pronounced and, I think, attractive French accent. When she was canvassing in Skegness in my Lincolnshire constituency during the last election an elderly lady said to her at her door: "You've got a funny accent. Do you come from Yorkshire?"

My wife was greatly flattered. She felt that she had finally arrived on the English political scene.

Cheryl Gillan MP
Member for Chesham and Amersham

When I was contesting Greater Manchester Central, my friend, and now researcher, Lynda MacKenzie, came up to help what was a virtual United Nations of canvassers on my team. We always liked to address each constituent by name, for example, "Good morning, Mrs Smith . . . Mr Jones . . . ."

In one street we came across a series of householders with Polish names. The French and American contingent had great difficulty with these and so Lynda, having run a ward with a large number of Polish members, took up the task of coaching them on approximate pronunciation, so they could greet each person without stumbling over the surname.

This was met with awe by one lad, who asked, "How come you can do this? Do you speak Communist?"

I hasten to add this took place before the era of glasnost!

The Rt Hon Sir William Clark

(MP for Croydon South 1974-92; for Surrey East 1970-74; and for Nottingham South 1959-66)

A Conservative candidate canvassing did not get a reply and left a card, which did not please the lady of the house when she returned. She telephoned the local Association and complained bitterly. The candidate on his card had written: "Sorry to have found you out."

Ann Widdecombe MP

Member for Maidstone, Under Secretary of State for Social Security

During the election campaign I produced a leaflet called "Standing up for Christian Principles" detailing my stand on moral and ethical issues. These were designed to be distributed outside church schools and on similarly appropriate occasions. However, they proved so popular that I took to ensuring that I always had a supply in my campaign car. On one occasion my Agent had just transferred a heap of literature from his car to mine and was driving away when I realised he had not left me any of these particular leaflets. Whereupon the very busy centre of Maidstone heard me hail frantically on my loudspeaker: "Brian! Come back! I haven't got any Christian principles."

Anything Goes

Stuart Sexton

Parliamentary Candidate for Workington, 1992

My poster campaign was extremely successful, bright blue with 'Vote Sexton', with the 'x' enlarged. I reckon I got at least another 500 votes when Labour supporters started tearing off the "ton".

Jacqui Lait MP

Member for Hastings and Rye

In a public meeting in one of the fishing villages in my constituency of Hastings and Rye, we were discussing serious subjects such as capital punishment and the effect of the European Community on the fishing industry.

A fisherman told us about some of the health regulations which apply to the fishing fleet. Fishing boats are regarded as commercial vehicles by the EC and as such are required to carry first aid kits, which is only wise and sensible. But recent regulation now requires the first aid kit to include two dozen condoms.

As the fisherman explained, it does not require a great deal of imagination to envisage the uses to which they can be put – on the masts, blown up as balloons, attached to the fishing nets . . . .

Lady Olga Maitland MP

Member for Sutton and Cheam

The popular time to canvass is usually between the hours of 6 and 9 pm. In Sutton, commuters arrive home tired and dusty and their first action when they get home is often to have a shower. I knocked on a door one evening and a handsome young man opened it with a towel around his waist. I concluded my "spiel" by offering him a leaflet. He stretched out to take it and his towel fell to the floor. What is the recommended etiquette for this, I wonder!

Gerald Howarth

(MP for Cannock and Burntwood 1983-92)

In our village there is a very staunch Labour supporter who had plastered posters of the Labour candidate on posts in her garden. On the final Sunday before voting I noticed that these had been overpasted with pictures of me taken from my Election Address. On returning from church I called at the newsagents where I was told that the said lady was extremely angry at this wanton vandalism. Much amused, I went to see her only to be told in no uncertain terms that such behaviour was beyond the pale and probably the work of a new Conservative branch which I had recently established. I soothed her with the thought that it was probably the work of some over-zealous Young Conservatives and went on my way.

As we were having lunch the young lady who babysits for us and lodges with the vicar and his wife appeared and so we invited her to stay for a cup of coffee. She seemed unusually mirthful and I enquired whether she had observed the political vandalism committed at the house of the Labour supporter. She had indeed. When I inquired if she knew who the perpetrator of this crime was she replied, "Well, it was like this. At about midnight last night the vicar said to me, 'have you seen all those Labour posters outside Mrs B's home? I dare you to go and paste Gerald's posters over them. Here's the paste, ready mixed, and the brush!' So off I went with the brush and photographs of you and pasted them on, ducking out of sight every time a car emerged from the entertainment at the village hall."

Although the vicar did not endorse me in any of his sermons, he found other ways to "go public". His sense of humour certainly gave me some encouragement and injected a little fun into the campaign.

Steven Norris MP

Member for Epping Forest

During the 1983 General Election in Oxford East, I was canvassing on the Bayswater Estate, which is not exactly the smartest part of town, and knocked on the door of a very normal semi-detached council house. I was met on the doorstep by every candidate's (male, that is) dream – a rather good-looking lady of indeterminate years in a white negligee.

"Yes?," she enquired, somewhat languidly.

"I'm Steve Norris," I said, "and I want to know whether I can count on your vote on election day?"

"You'd better come in," she said.

What could I say? Never one to turn up the opportunity of a "conversion", I did exactly as she suggested! As I walked into the living room I was struck by the somewhat unusual decor. The entire room was furnished in black leather from ceiling to floor, including a number of rather large and extremely comfortable settees – not to mention the odd pouffe.

On one of these lounged another extremely desirable resident of the Borough, this time clad in an equally fetching diaphanous black number. Next to her on the couch was a large African gentleman in a pure white suit, black shirt, white tie and more rings than a large gas cooker.

"What can I do for you, son?" he asked.

"Well," I said, "I'm Steve Norris, and I'm asking for your vote at the next General Election."

"Conservative are you?"

"Well, of course," I said.

"Oh, that's all right, son. We're all in favour of small business round here, aren't we, girls?"

David Porter MP

Member for Waveney

Although it was one of the rare days in the 1992 campaign when the heavens hadn't opened on us, it was still "one of those days".

In the morning I was told I wouldn't be getting a particular vote in a rural area because I "hadn't said anything nice about that Colonel Gaddafi".

In the afternoon the team had to push the campaign bus out of a muddy lane and the American photo-journalist who was with us, covering the campaign for a book comparing the British and American election of '92, announced he'd lost a reel of film of the unrepeatable visit to the Lowestoft fish market.

By the end of the evening in one of my town areas, I was looking forward to meeting the rest of the team in a local hostelry. The local councillor and I decided to make one last call as it was getting dark.

There was a low light in the lounge, but none in the hall. We rang the bell twice and received no response, so I headed for the gate. My friend peered in the window.

"Oh my goodness!" His cry froze me in my tracks. "There's a couple on the settee!" I guessed he didn't mean they were watching TV, so I carried on swiftly to the gate.

However, the lounge window opened and a furious woman draped in the curtain appeared. I reluctantly returned to the scene to make excuses.

As soon as she saw who we were she apologised profusely for not having a front door key to let us in!

I was grateful that my councillor didn't offer to see she was knocked up in polling day!

Sir Albert McQuarrie

Ayr Constituency, Branch Member

During the General Election campaign in the Ayr Constituency, I elected to erect some 300 posters for Phil Gallie on lamposts. I had almost reached the end of the job and had climbed some twenty feet in Bentinck Drive, Troon when I was approached by a female (I couldn't call her lady as it turns out!) who told me in no uncertain manner that I could not put up the posters on the lampost opposite her home. I told her I had every right to do so and she became quite irate. I noticed her windows were plastered with posters in support of the Labour Candidate. I suggested to her that this was the reason why she did not want Tory posters facing her base. She agreed and demanded that either I remove the Tory ones just erected or she would do so after I had gone. I, therefore, climbed a further five feet and added two more posters to the lampost, assuring her that if they were removed I would come each day and put up more and more, as Phil Gallie was going to win by our efforts. She responded with the comment, "Youse have nae chance at all."

As I walked off smiling I said, "Wait and see."

I saw her dejected figure at the count when we held the seat against all the odds and now have a fine MP to follow Lord Younger.

Climbing twenty feet up a ladder three hundred times to tie posters on lamposts and doing the same to take them down again was not a bad effort for a 74½ year old Knight of the Realm and True Blue Tory to inspire our supporters.

Lady Olga Maitland MP
Member for Sutton and Cheam

I was canvassing one house in my constituency which is of somewhat doubtful repute. The door opened to show a man wearing only his trousers. As I was about to launch into my patter a woman's voice yelled down from upstairs, "Don't worry about him, dear, he's only here occasionally!"

David Douglas

Agent and Secretary, Hornsey and Wood Green Conservative Association

The Royal British Legion held a Cockney Evening during the Election, to which all the candidates duly turned up. The Labour Mayor and Mayoress were in full pearly outfit and the Labour candidate was asked to pose for the local paper. Our candidate, Andrew Boff, alert as ever, sauntered up behind the Labour candidate while the photographs were taken.

A week passed and the paper was printed, but no pictures of the Labour candidate were in at all. The photographer later told me that Andrew had raised his fingers to make her appear to have "bunny ears". This sabotage not only ruined their week's publicity, it gave us a marvellous memento of the Election.

David Amess MP

Member for Basildon

One afternoon we were canvassing in a low rise block of flats with entryphones for senior citizens. We eventually got into the block and an elderly lady was delighted to see me. "Thank Gawd it's you Mr Amess – God Bless the Conservative Party," she said. "Of course 'Im in there – ee's rank Labour but can hardly get out of his chair! 'Ee thinks I've applied for a postal vote for him – well I didn't – that's one less for the other lot!"

Sir Richard Body MP
Member for Holland with Boston

A new recruit to our canvassing team, who came from what might be described as the best part of town, as well dressed as she was well educated, was asked to deliver our election broadsheet on a housing estate she had never previously visited.

The first people she saw were two women emerging from a shop, cursing, in picturesque language she had seldom heard before, about the cost of living.

Plucking up courage, she nervously murmured, "I hope you won't throw tomatoes at me if I give you this."

"Nah, duck, we're bloody Tories."

With Friends Like That . . .

Robert Banks MP
Member for Harrogate

Whilst I was canvassing during the last Election, an old lady earnestly said to me: "Oh Mr Banks I always support the Conservative Party, but I never vote . . . ."

Hartley Booth MP
Member for Finchley

It is always wonderful to have supporters coming forward during an Election to put up Conservative posters, although there is a risk they may end up in surprising places.

One poster was seen on the back of a constituent's van all over Finchley during the last Election. The poster declared "I'm voting Booth" on a fine blue background. Beneath the poster was the name of the van owner's firm: "North London Pest Control".

Nicholas Winterton MP

Member for Macclesfield

Having been up from dawn until dusk for weeks, day after day, in a hectic round of speeches, canvassing and leafleting, you will imagine my surprise when I read in a local paper just a few days before Polling Day, that I was so confident of victory that I would be "on holiday during the vital days leading up to Polling Day".

If only it were true, my beleaguered campaign team moaned, as the lawyers' writs flew!

The scurrilous rag in question apologised publicly, unreservedly, eventually, but the damage was done. No candidate can expect his supporters to turn out in the wet and the wind to vote for him if they have been told he is off sunning himself elsewhere.

Martin Graham

Deputy Director, Conservative Research Department

Central Office had a bomb scare during the Election. About 250 of us were bundled out into Smith Square – some without jackets – on a cold, windy March day. Next, we were moved out of the square itself, as the whole area was cordonned off.

Three of us, thinking of Christmas Day in the First World War, decided to seek shelter in the Liberal Democrat HQ round the corner. Fraternising with the enemy turned out to be very pleasant, and the Liberal staff were most hospitable.

As we left, half-an-hour later, the Liberal receptionist said: "Oh, you'd better take these." He handed me about 400 letters, mostly addressed to Chris Patten – many of them in response to a fund-raising appeal. The local postman, faced with a cordonned-off Smith Square, had decided (in his infinite wisdom) to leave the Conservative Party's morning post in the next best place.

Roger Knapman MP

Member for Stroud

D uring the course of the last campaign I visited a street with only one poster suggesting that the occupants were to favour the Liberal Democrat cause. While I was canvassing other houses in the street, a man approached me with his wife some steps behind.

He told me that he proposed to vote Conservative; I thanked him and asked where he lived; he pointed to the house displaying the Liberal Democrat poster.

He then introduced me to his wife; I said I was sorry she was a Liberal Democrat and asked why she was going to vote that way. She also assured me that she was going to vote Conservative. I then asked who else lived in the house and they said: "Just the two of us."

After a while it dawned on me that I should ask, in that case, why they were displaying a Liberal Democrat poster. He answered, "Well, I have ambitions to be a District Councillor and they tell me that the most likely way of becoming a Councillor in this district is to stand for the Liberal Democrats."

Madron Seligman MEP

Member for Sussex West

The Chairman of my association wrote and asked Central Office for a list of MEP's broken down by age and sex. The answer he got was, "We find most of them are broken down by alcohol rather than sex."

Iain Mills MP

Member for Meriden

My calling card for the election had a picture of my wife, myself and our two rather pretty glossy labradors. It elicited various remarks, for instance:

"I might not vote for the man but I will for the bow-wows," and:

"Which out of the three dogs is the candidate?"

Laurence Robertson

Parliamentary Candidate for Ashfield, 1992

There is, of course, much rivalry between the Parties as regards posting and fly-posting. My colleagues stuck some posters up along a member's farm land but unfortunately ran three trees over, which constituted fly-posting. After the Labour Party had complained, my colleagues – two ladies – went to take them down.

On arriving at the site, they got out of their car and began to take the posters down. The driver of a passing car – moving at around 60 mph – saw these apparent vandals pulling posters down and, intent on remonstrating, screeched to a halt – only for the car behind to smash into the back of him!

He shouted furiously at the driver behind and at the people taking the posters down. It was only then that he saw that the parked car, belonging to the supposed vandals, was covered in blue posters.

Maggie McEwen

Agent and Secretary for Brentwood and Ongar Conservative Association

Those familiar with the procedure of the count will know that a point is reached where all the candidates and their agents are called into the centre to examine the spoilt ballot papers and argue about their validity.

On the occasion of the last Election, we were all gathered heads down, haggling over the ticks and circles when we came across one which carried a signature. "Ah," I exclaimed, "disqualified for recognition."

Being the only professional Agent there, no one else had known until that moment what they were looking for, but now they were all eager to find another paper which carried an indication of the elector's identity.

Finally, my candidate held one up in triumph. Across the paper in very large letters was written, "Bollocks". "Disqualified for recognition," he said. "This is my Agent's handwriting!"

Edward Garnier MP

Member for Harborough

In the 1983 Election my job on the last day and in the final hours of the Election Day itself was to collect promised voters from their houses. About fifteen minutes before the close of polling I knocked on the door of a couple who had promised to vote for us – according to our canvass return.

The young wife appeared at the door to say that whilst she would be delighted to vote for the Conservative Party she couldn't leave the house because her husband was in the bath and it was the children's bedtime. After some desperate talking, I managed to persuade both her and her husband to come out and vote on the promise that I would look after the children in the car while they went in to vote.

Mission accomplished, or so I thought. As soon as the parents had disappeared into the polling station, their five-year-old son popped up from the back seat and said, "Do you like Mrs Thatcher?" Needless to say, I gave her my full approval, only to be told by the wretched child, "My Mum and Dad can't stand her." So that was a wasted effort!

The Rt Hon the Viscount Whitelaw

(MP for Penrith and Border 1955-83, Chairman of the Conservative Party 1955-83, Deputy Leader of the Conservative Party 1975-91)

I was canvassing in Nairn in the north of Scotland, where I, myself, was brought up. I shook hands with a young man and said, "I am Willie Whitelaw. I hope you will vote for our Conservative candidate." His rather surprising reply was, "Oh I know all about you, I am very grateful because you have done a lot for the Golf Greenkeepers Association." I am incidentally, President of this Association.

Having established this connection, I said again, "I trust you will vote for our Conservative candidate."

"Certainly not," he said, "I am going to vote for the Scottish Nationalists!"

Lady Olga Maitland MP

Member for Sutton and Cheam

Out canvassing one evening, I gave my usual speech although the door was only ajar. A knarled hand came through in a rude gesture. I recoiled and then came a croaking voice from behind the door, "That's two votes, my husband and myself!"

James Fuke

North Western Area, Conservative Central Office

At a briefing meeting for Voluntary Workers, the Deputy Central Office Agent did a session on NCRs – a system for marking off the Electoral Register. Having extolled the virtues of the system, given a practical demonstration of how NCRs are used from the canvassing returns coming in to deliveries and knocking up, the session came to a close.

"Are there any questions?" asked the Deputy.

"Yes," said a lady of advanced years, sitting in the front row. "Can you ask that bloody Agent of ours to produce copies of the Electoral Register with bigger print; my eyes aren't what they used to be and I can't see the names for crossing off."

Julian Lewis

Deputy Director of the Conservative Research Department

A week before election day was announced, Jack Straw, the Labour education spokesman, appeared on *Newsnight*. He was just gearing up to denounce our book of Labour MPs' quotations, *Who's Left?*, as a "descent into the gutter and almost into the sewer". But interviewer Peter Snow stopped him in his tracks.

SNOW: Jack Straw, you apparently saluted the courage and determination of anti-nuclear protestors at Greenham Common. That all right? Did you say that?

STRAW: I – it depends what date it was – I can't remember – it's a very long time ago.

SNOW: I will tell you – Early Day Motion number 609, July 1982. Anything wrong with the Tories saying that about you?

STRAW: I don't mind – it's a matter of public record.

The same confusion reigned when we exposed the fact that Labour candidates' official biographies had been doctored to cover-up their genuine entries as members of CND. Some claimed they had left the organisation just before the biographies were printed. Others admitted that they were still paid-up members. And Neil Kinnock declared, quite wrongly, that "nothing at all" had been altered.

After the election, an interview in the *Independent* with one of Labour's new MPs began as follows:

"Oh yes," Lynne Jones says, as she scrutinises a copy of her entry in Labour's General Election candidates' directory. "This is where they [Labour HQ] deleted the reference to me being a member of CND."

John Watson

(MP for Skipton and Ripon, 1979-1987)

A helper in 1979 was driving from Skipton to Barnolds-wick. A sign advertising a local pub said, "A pie, a pint and a friendly word."

My friend entered the pub. He ordered a pie and a pint. They were delivered in silence.

"What about the friendly word?" he asked.

"Don't eat the pie," said the landlord.

Curiouser and Curiouser

The Hon Timothy Sainsbury MP
Member for Hove, Minister for Trade

During the recent General Election, a parcel was delivered by hand to the Campaign HQ in Hove. It had been sealed with a great deal of sellotape, carried no indication of its place of origin and had a handwritten address.

The Agent placed it on her desk for sorting. Before action could be taken, Tim Sainsbury, the Candidate, entered the room, rummaged through the post and found the brown package, approx 12 x 6 inches in size. Having watched the video on security, his thoughts immediately registered "very suspicious". He picked up the parcel, examined it, turned it over and over, sniffed it, handed it to the Agent, with the words: "Should we call the Police?"

The Agent looked at it, turned it over, examined it and returned it gallantly to her Candidate with the reply: "Perhaps."

With that, Mr Sainsbury ceremoniously carried the "bomb" to the recently refurbished disabled toilets at the back of the building, stating to all and sundry: "No one is to use the disabled loo. It may have a bomb in it!"

The Police were duly called. Excitement at last in Hove! A PC and WPC arrived and were escorted to the loo. The PC picked up the "bomb", turned it over and over several times, handed it to the WPC, who repeated the process.

The PC declared that he would open it himself, carefully. With bated breath the Agent and WPC stood at a suitably safe distance.

The explosion that followed shook the building with laughter for several minutes. Our "bomb" contained hundreds of cards, advertising the oldest profession, which had been left in telephone kiosks. A genuine complaint by a constituent!

Richard Wilkinson

Parliamentary Candidate for Kilmarnock and Loudoun, 1992

The *Kilmarnock Standard* gave me a lot of excellent publicity during my candidacy. In May it ran a short story saying I apparently spent more on purchasing rosettes than did the Liberal Democrat candidate in her whole campaign. My thirty-six rosettes cost my understanding Treasurer £34. Meanwhile, apparently, the entire Liberal Democrat campaign cost £22.49.

Keith Simpson

Parliamentary Candidate for Plymouth Devonport, 1992

During the second week of the campaign I was out canvassing with a small team of stalwarts in the ward nearest to Devonport dockyard. That day the USS *Guadacanal*, an American helicopter-carrier, had docked on a goodwill visit. News of the arrival of this ship had attracted a large number of "ladies of the night". They had positioned themselves at strategic points just outside the dockyard to give a warm welcome to our American allies.

So, just as we began our canvass several hundred American sailors appeared on the streets looking for a good "run ashore". Friendly and good natured, they kept stopping us to ask whether it was "party time", given our rosettes and badges. Considerable time was wasted explaining that we were out canvassing – not "knocking up" as this has a quite different connotation in America. My constituency chairman proved to be very popular as he cheerily pointed the Americans in the right direction for entertainment and refreshment. Having run the gauntlet of American inquisitiveness we then had some lively repartee with the visiting ladies.

As I was driven away in a car festooned with "Vote Keith Simpson" and Conservative posters, we found ourselves stationary at a busy road junction. I was anxious that we should move on as out of the corner of my eye I could see one of the ladies approaching our car. Candidates will frequently do anything to get elected, but being accused of kerb crawling is not one of them!

James Costello

Deputy Central Office Agent

An Agent was warned by a colleague, in the run up to the General Election, that a "nutter" was heading his way. Apparently this chap had a habit of standing against famous politicians and either changing his name by deed poll so that he had the same name as them or calling himself the Conservative Party Candidate.

On hearing this the Agent immediately contacted the Returning Officer, and asked that he be informed immediately if a nomination paper was lodged by this man so that action could be taken. The Returning Officer reassured him that he would do so.

When 12 noon on the last day for lodging nominations had passed the Agent rang the RO for the names of persons nominated and said that as he had heard nothing about the "nutter" he assumed he had not bothered to lodge a paper after all. The RO said that he had in fact appeared but there was nothing to worry about. The man had come to the RO at 11.00 am that day. On the form he described himself as "The Conservative Party Candidate". The RO, a wily old bird, decided that there were more ways than one to skin a cat. He said, "I was just about to have some tea, would you care to join me before we get down to the boring old paper work?" The man readily agreed and the whole process of ordering and consuming the tea and biscuits took an inordinately long period of time.

As they were drinking their tea and chatting away in friendly fashion the RO said, "I see you have described yourself as the Conservative Party Candidate on your paper. That cannot be right. You are not the famous MP in this constituency." The man agreed but said nevertheless he could describe himself in any way he chose. The RO replied confidently that the local Tories would take out an injunction to stop him from using this description but they would be powerless to do anything if he simply called himself "Conservative". He emphasised this last part pointedly, just stopping short of giving a nudge and a wink. Then, with greatly exaggerated movements, he laid a pen on the table and said he was just leaving the room for a moment.

On his return, at 11.58, he saw that the nomination paper had been altered as discussed. He said they had chatted long enough and it was time to get down to business. The man replied in the affirmative when asked if he was now ready officially to lodge his nomination paper. The RO picked it up for scrutiny, as if he had never seen it before. Shaking his head sadly he informed the gentleman he could not accept this nomination as it had been altered and was therefore not valid!

Peter Morton

Acting Agent, Portsmouth South Conservative Association

Two ladies were canvassing down the one side of a terraced street and sharing the same canvass card. One looked at the card to tell the other the names of the electors at her next house, number 20.

"Richard Wilson, Christine Wilson and Samantha Wilson," she said, adding flippantly, "father bear, mother bear and baby bear."

As she rang the bell of number 22 she heard the door of number 20 open and her friend say to the resident, "Good evening Mr Bear, I'm canvassing on behalf of your Conservative candidate David Martin . . ."

Graham Robb

Parliamentary Candidate for Hartlepool, 1992

On one of the roughest council estates in Hartlepool, a fellow came to the door. He was a huge man, string vest and all – a seriously big lad, the kind who could crack walnuts with his eyelids. He told me where to go (quite unambiguously), explaining that he ate Tories for breakfast. I almost believed him. All the more so when, walking back down his garden path, I saw a pile of very large bones lying there. It occurred to me that these could very well be the remains of a former Tory canvasser.

I knocked on the next door. The fellow said: "Yes Mr Robb, I'll be delighted to support you, but can you do something about my neighbour? He's on remand for stealing from the abattoir."

John Redwood MP

Member for Wokingham, Minister of State for the Environment

Whilst canvassing one evening, I rang a doorbell at about the time of the early evening news. A rather cross elector came to the door looking harrassed. I explained to him I was the local Conservative Parliamentary Candidate. Before I could get any further he exploded, "I haven't got time to talk to you. I want to hear about the election and it's on telly at the moment." Without more ado he shut the door. I was left saying through the letterbox, "But I'm the election here." All to no avail. Such is the power of television.

David Evans MP

Member for Welwyn Hatfield

At the time of the General Election, Welwyn Hatfield had had a Labour controlled District Council for thirteen years and in view of the anticipated slump in the Liberal Democrat vote, Labour felt they had a real chance of winning Welwyn Hatfield, as they had twice in 1974.

At the count the tables were laid out for the three parties' individual votes to be stacked after counting. Two thirds of the way through the count, proceedings came to an abrupt halt. After making enquiries my Agent, Paul Burrett, came over to me and said that there was a delay because it had been necessary to send out for another table to put my votes on!

From that moment on I had the most enjoyable hour of my life as I realised that not only would we enjoy a handsome victory in Welwyn Hatfield but also a stunning victory nationally.

Andrew Robathan MP

Member for Blaby

The first time I canvassed for myself was in Fulham, in the Council elections of 1990. I rang the intercom for an upstairs flat and, when it was answered, said: "This is Andrew Robathan, your Conservative candidate in the Council elections."

"No it isn't," said a youngish female voice, "you are A——— B———. Come on in."

The door opened and up I went . . . to be greeted by a very attractive girl of about 21, with a towel wrapped around her, and wearing nothing else.

She looked startled.

"Well I did tell you," I said.

"Yes."

"May I count on your support on May 3rd?"

"Oh definitely!"

I could not see any reasonable way of continuing the conversation, so left – probably just as well, as I met the said A--- B---, and a friend, by the front gate. They worked for Central Office.

Jane Emmerson

Parliamentary Candidate for Bethnal Green and Stepney, 1992

Sometimes a local solution can be found. One morning I was canvassing in the constituency and called on a Mrs Smith.

"Hello – I'm Jane Emmerson, your Conservative candidate for the General Election. I'm visiting everyone to ask them for their support and to see if I can be of any help."

"Oh!" Mrs Smith replied, "I've been waiting for you! I want to know what you're going to do about all this wastage in the NHS?"

I proceeded to tell Mrs Smith how the Conservatives had tackled this problem by introducing NHS Trusts and GP contracts and that Mr Major's new policies would change things for the better.

"I know all that love! What I want to know is, what you're going to do about me spare legs? I've got one on and two spare! Years love – 'ad 'em years – and they've never been to collect 'em yet! Will you take 'em? They're in the back cupboard!"

Somewhat surprised I said to her that I would do what I could to help and contact the health authority for her.

I then crossed the road to canvass a twenty-storey tower block. Taking the lift to the top floor I knocked on the first door and a man in a wheel chair, wearing a string vest and very little else appeared. I told him who I was, asked him if he would vote for me and did he need any help.

"Yes – I want a flat on the ground floor. I can't get me wheelchair in the lift! Me wife's playing hell because she's having to run after me day and night – it's bloody appalling love – bloody appalling!" He then went on to say, "But – I'll tell you something – I'm not the only one around here that's got a problem. There's Harry two floors down – he's only got one leg. Then there's Tom, below him, he's got no legs at all! So – what you going to do about that then? Tell me – you politicians reckon you know it all – give me an answer to that then!"

I looked at him and replied, "You want to get round to Mrs Smith over in Bethnal Green Road. She will be pleased to see you. She's got some spare legs she's desperate to get rid of!"

Mary Gibbon
Parliamentary Candidate for Wallsend, 1992

A local TV programme called "Points of Order" goes out at 11.40 pm on a Thursday evening (Tyne Tees TV). Representatives from each political party are invited to go along to debate a particular issue. This time the topic was education and I – as a teacher – was invited onto the programme. It was my first TV appearance; I was a little nervous but keen to learn and gain from the experience.

I took my seat as instructed and sat well back in my chair, in order to give the impression of confidence, only to find that my feet were dangling about a foot from the floor. (I should mention that I am 5 feet 2 inches tall.)

I said that I hoped that the cameramen would avoid my legs as I'd hate it to be said that the Conservative didn't have her feet on the ground! Laughter from the crew. They fetched a box and the programme was recorded with my feet resting on it. So it wasn't just the PM who used a soapbox during this election!

Michael Mates MP
Member for Hampshire East, Minister of State for Northern Ireland

While canvassing a council estate in the constituency, I called at a house and was greeted by a lady who told me that she would be supporting me. I asked whether this included her husband and was told that he was away and unable to vote, since he was a serving a sentence in the local prison. I commiserated with her and passed on.

Three or four houses later I had the same experience: promise of support but regret that the man of the house was detained at Her Majesty's pleasure and would be unable to contribute to the Conservative cause. With the same expressions of regret and commiseration I moved on.

At the end of the estate I met an irate man who ranted for several minutes about the iniquities of our party's law and order policies. Having listened to this as patiently as I could I was unable to forbear from striking the knock-down blow, "Well we can't be all that bad. At least two of your neighbours are paying the price for their crimes!"

Stuart Sexton

Parliamentary Candidate for Workington, 1992

Much of my constituency is rural Lake District; talking to the farmers is essential. I was invited to take the rostrum at the Cockermouth sheep auctions.

They started bidding!

John Carlisle MP

Member for Luton North

Some say election campaigns are too long. For others, they're clearly not quite long enough. One lady in Luton on whom I called was so undecided as to where she would cast her vote on Polling Day that she said she would be walking instead of taking her car so that she would have longer to make up her mind!

Anthony Nelson MP

Member for Chichester, Economic Secretary to the Treasury

The turning point in the Conservative Party's political prospects came for me while canvassing in a small village just north of Chichester. I was on my way to visit the sub-post office when a manhole cover was raised and up popped a sewage worker. "Are you the Tory candidate?" he asked. I said I was. "Mind if I ask you a question? Are you for or against fox hunting?" Rather apprehensively I replied that I was in favour of fox hunting. "That's all right then, you can count on my vote," and he disappeared back down into the sewer. I knew then that if the sewage workers were behind us, all was not lost. Believe it or not the name of the village was Lavant!

Graham Smith

Constituency Finance Advisor, Conservative Central Office

The night "they" decided to include the Labour Party's telephone number in a *Conservative* election broadcast will long be remembered by members of the team engaged at Conservative Central Office during the General Election to answer telephone calls from members of the general public.

Not only did it bring an immediate response from Labour supporters who rang in to express their disquiet (to put it very mildly) but it also encouraged a reaction on the part of

Labour Party Headquarters in Walworth Road, hitherto unpublished.

One of the team at Central Office actually telephoned the number at Walworth Road, as suggested in the broadcast, and was told: "Sorry but we are playing the Tories at their own game. We've sent everyone home and they won't be back until 10.30 tomorrow morning. What's more, the *Daily Mirror* is going to publish a suggestion to call their number."

The public quickly responded to the *Mirror's* idea. The phones did not stop from morning to night with call after call expressing views in a language best described as being "Anglo Saxon".

Amongst the callers was one who was very irate and who obviously had a serious problem. I talked to him about the broadcast and it became obvious that he had not even seen it, but was responding to the *Mirror's* suggestion to telephone us. He ended up by saying to me: "And do you know what upset me most? You gave out *our* telephone number!"

Laurence Robertson

Parliamentary Candidate for Ashfield, 1992

One gentleman phoned me to talk about the local Conservative Club. "Oh," I said, trying to be pleasant, "it's a nice club; I'm a member too, you know."

"Well then," he replied, "you tell me why the president's wife spat at me last Saturday?"

Angela Knight MP

Member for Erewash

I was addressing a public meeting during the election campaign and when it came to questions there was one member of the audience for whom everything was wrong. He was complaining about interest rates, VAT, national insurance, his business rates, the community charge, etc. After having fielded the first half dozen, I realised that he was in business and so I asked him if trade was bad. He replied, "Business has never been better. I haven't noticed a recession at all."

"What is your business?" I asked him.

His reply: "Government surplus."

Robert Adley MP

Member for Christchurch

From 1970-74 I represented a seat called Bristol North East which has long since been chopped up into bits of four other constituencies one of which is the present Kingswood division. During the last election campaign, I spent a day with Rob Hayward in part of my old constituency. I knocked on a door in Mangotsfield and was greeted by a charming elderly lady who said, "Hello Mr Adley. Nice to see you. Haven't seen you around here for quite some time."

As it was eighteen years since I represented her, it is clear that the news of my departure had not yet filtered through to her!

Mary Gibbon

Parliamentary Candidate for Wallsend, 1992

Several cabinet ministers visited the North East during the election. When this happened about four or five candidates whose constituencies were in or around Newcastle joined a walkabout in the city centre.

On one occasion we had had a very successful morning with Kenneth Baker, the then Home Secretary; we afterwards all went to a local hostelry on the quayside for lunch with him, his adviser and his security men. He was instantly recognised and then suddenly the place emptied. Kenneth Baker burst out laughing and said, "They've just realised that the police are here!" We'd obviously disturbed the drinking session of some local villains!

James Mackie

Vice Chairman, Clackmannan Constituency Conservative Association

During the Council elections in 1990, I was putting up my posters on lamposts in a former mining village near Stirling where I had once served as a police constable. While I was balancing on top of a ladder putting up a blue coloured poster one of the locals asked what I was doing. I explained, to which he enquired as to which party I was representing.

"Is it not rather obvious?" I said to him.

To which he replied, "I know you're a blue-nosed bastard, but what party are you standing for – Labour or the SNP?"

In the Eye of the Beholder

The Rt Hon Douglas Hurd MP

Member for Witney, Secretary of State for Foreign and Commonwealth Affairs

Potential electors cannot be placed in little boxes and labelled by categories. We are a people – thank heavens – of infinite variety and eccentricity, to be approached with humanity by pollsters, sociologists and advertising agencies.

Canvassing down a high street, it was somewhat disarming to find that the young punk in black leather and one earring turned out to be a computer analyst with deeply orthodox Conservative opinions. My next encounter was with an elegant old lady, who promptly moved away in fierce left-wing disgust. The life-long Liberal then promised me his vote because of his Party's hostility to fox hunting!

These characters will never be picked up and classified. Real conversation with real people is the essence of a democratic election. They are both refreshing and chastening to the professional politician.

Walter Sweeney MP

Member for The Vale of Glamorgan

After the election was over, my majority of 19 (the smallest in the Commons) was a talking point. All MPs have received letters from constituents which begin: "I have been a Conservative, Labour, Liberal voter all my life, but . . ." I receive letters beginning: "Was I one of the 19?"

When I first took my seat in the House, two Tory Knights of the Shires were comparing notes on their election campaigns. One said that his majority had been 13, and the other that his majority had been 17. He then turned to me, saying, "And how did you get on, young man?"

I replied "19", whereupon both gentleman looked suitably impressed and congratulated me. What they did not realise was that while they had been referring to their majorities in thousands, my majority was literally 19.

Madron Seligman MEP

Member for Sussex West

Overheard about a candidate who liked to meet the electors, and who did a lot of walkabouts during the campaign: "He shook the hand of 30% of the electorate, and shook the confidence of the rest."

Angela Knight MP

Member for Erewash

I was in the middle of Ilkeston during the Election and an elderly gentleman came up to me, took me by the hand, started pumping it up and down and said, "It's lovely to meet you, me 'duck'. A've been a Labour supporter all me life, and nothing's gonna change me now, but I 'opes you win."

Glyn Môn Hughes

Parliamentary Candidate for Birkenhead, 1992

From my name, you might guess that I am a Welshman. I was born, however, in what is known as the capital of Wales and Ireland – Liverpool. During the campaign BBC Wales decided it would do a series of interviews with Welsh people standing in English seats and visited Croydon, Hereford, Ribble Valley – and Birkenhead. I suggested they came to a house meeting on my schedule – but hadn't realised the interview would be fully in Welsh. That was all right for me, but it's difficult to keep a straight face when I am nodding in agreement with the interviewer and my supporters are shaking their heads, understanding not one word of the conversation.

The Lord Archer of Weston-Super-Mare

(Deputy Chairman of the Conservative Party 1985-86)

The Communist candidate in Sheffield, Ms T Clifford shouted at Jeffrey Archer in the market square while he was on a walkabout canvassing for Irvine Patnick.

"Archer, you are a Tory scab and a fascist pig, a mass murderer and what is worse you are a friend of John Major's."

Jeffrey couldn't think of a suitable reply.

The Communist candidate polled 99 votes and Mr Patnick was returned to the House of Commons with a swing of only 0.7% against him.

The Rt Hon Nicholas Scott MP

Member for Chelsea, Minister of State at the Department of Social Security

On one of my several election tours I tentatively enquired in the course of covering six Yorkshire marginal seats about the impact of the recession on the county. One of the Association chairmen turned to me and said in broad Yorkshire: "Mr Scott, the only companies in trouble up here are subsidiaries of southern companies."

Sir William van Straubenzee

(MP for Wokingham 1959-87)

I was canvassing in that part of Bracknell which is the oldest part and which was actually being built when I was first adopted for the then Wokingham Constituency in

1957. It follows that a number of the electors, having lived there all their adult lives, had, as it were, grown up both with me and the town.

One such was a charming lady who, coming to the door and recognizing me, said with a gleaming smile, "Good gracious, are you our candidate again?"

I tell Andrew Mackay, the outstandingly good MP for East Berkshire, that she looked very disappointed when I told her the truth. I fear however that is but poetic licence.

James Gray

Parliamentary Candidate for Ross, Cromarty and Skye, 1992

As a first-time candidate in the 1992 General Election, I was very well aware of what a lowly figure I was in Conservative politics. My ego was therefore greatly boosted by a phone call from the BBC one Friday afternoon to ask if I would be interviewed live on *Newsnight*, an honour usually reserved for Ministers, coveted by backbenchers and unheard of for lowly Parliamentary Candidates.

My ego was further boosted by the fact that the programme had seemed to go without a hitch; and feeling pretty pleased with myself as I left the studio I was ecstatic with self-esteem when a small boy came up and asked for my autograph. I duly signed, remembering to ask his name first to personalise the message. He looked at what I had written, obviously deciphering my illegible signature, and looked up:

"Got a rubber?" he asked.

Martin Winter

Parliamentary Candidate for Tooting, 1992

Overheard at the start of the election: two Labour supporters discussing their redistribution of wealth policies. One was older and clearly more experienced.

The younger one said, "Does that mean if you have two houses you will give me one?"

"Of course it does," said the older.

"And does it mean that if you have two cars you would give me one?"

"Exactly so."

"And if you had two video cameras, would you give me one?" persisted the younger.

The older one's face became furrowed. "How did you know I had two video cameras?" he said crossly.

Irvine Patnick MP

Member for Sheffield Hallam, Lord Commissioner of the Treasury

While canvassing in a less than picturesque part of Hallam during the General Election I received a two finger gesture from the occupants of a passing car. When the car had to stop at some traffic lights I had the opportunity to say, "I take it both votes are for me then."

Andrew Lansley

Director, Conservative Research Department

Central Office had its work cut out organising two or three press conferences _per day_ during the campaign. Often, Saatchi and Saatchi would design large posters specially for the day. They would be pasted onto large screens, either side of the platform.

One morning, the first theme of the day was Defence. A particularly good poster depicted Conservative defence policy in terms of a hoarding-sized hedgehog with spines – and Labour defence policy in terms of a hedgehog (courtesy of trick photography) without spines.

So far, so good. But shortly before the second press conference it was realised that the day's poster might present a problem. The second theme was none other than animal welfare!

The journalists arrived to see the poster sites covered with freshly-pasted light blue paper. None of them twigged!

Richard Spring MP

Member for Bury St Edmunds

I was about to enter a shop in Newmarket High Street when a lady in a tightly knotted headscarf stopped me to wish me well. She came from a village called Six Mile Bottom, just outside Newmarket, in my friend Jim Paice's constituency. She told me she had recently come out of hospital and when her son first visited her there, she asked him to bring her a framed photograph of her racehorse. It was duly delivered. An astonished nurse, expressed surprise that she should prefer to gaze upon a horse, rather than her family. "In fact," she told the nurse, "I much prefer horses to humans." Her reply clearly amazed the nurse even more. "If you can afford to own a racehorse," asked the nurse, "Why don't you go to a private hospital?" "Well," came the reply, "it is precisely because I own a racehorse that I could never ever afford to go privately."

The Rt Hon John Major MP
The Prime Minister
Member for Huntingdon

During the General Election campaign I visited Luton town centre for what was supposed to be a brief walkabout, followed by the first outing for the soap box. When we arrived, we found the Socialist Workers Party out in force. We plunged into the crowd. There was a lot of pushing and some fairly colourful language, in the best traditions of the hustings. A small malodorous element was intent on causing trouble. My detectives were looking increasing anxious. Then, bursting out of the crowd towards me, came a very large man. Crew cut. Tattoos. Bulging neck. Dirty tee-shirt. Hairy chest. Shouting unintelligibly as he came closer. The detectives tensed. I tensed. There was no way out. He got right up to me, seized my hand and shouted: "Good on yer, John. Best of luck."

Richard Ottaway MP

Member for Croydon South

D uring the election campaign a colour photograph of myself was distributed throughout the constituency. Although I am rather unphotogenic, it wasn't a bad effort, and I was fairly pleased with the end result. However, my optimism was quickly dashed when a lady walked up to me holding the photograph. She took one look at me, then the photograph, and said, "It's amazing what these photographers can do nowadays," and walked off.

Julian Davidson

Parliamentary Candidate for Yeovil, 1992

L ife was rarely dull in Yeovil during the 1992 campaign. There were a number of stories which helped keep attention at public meetings.

One concerned a famous Liberal who was late for a fleeting appearance in the constituency during an election campaign. A restless gathering in a village hall had been waiting for more than half an hour when he eventually arrived in a flurry of apologies. Racing to the stage he paused only to turn to his research assistant and say, "Give me the fifteen minute speech." She dutifully rummaged in some papers and produced the speech.

Stepping on to the platform, he went on to deliver his speech which went on . . . and on . . . and on . . . and on. With the crowd getting restless and most of the back row asleep, he eventually stopped after _fifty_ minutes. There was understandably subdued applause. As he left rapidly for the next engagement, he turned on his research assistant and said, "I told you to give me the fifteen minute speech," to which she replied, "I did, but I gave you three copies!"

Brian Cummins
Northavon Branch Member

We were in Nepal on April 9th and the next day, when we were climbing a hill I asked a local farmer who was clutching a radio to his ear the results of the General Election. He told me that the Party of Liberation had won by some 30 votes with a slim overall majority. There were certain members in our group who took this as a demonstration of Mr Kinnock's success. I kept my own counsel. Their mortification and my delight was therefore more extreme the following day and some thousands of feet higher when an Australian assured us that John Major was back in power.

Pam Smith
Chairman of Yorkshire Area Conservatives

"No luv, we're all Labour here."
I was canvassing on a large housing estate in Leeds and a middle-aged looking man had answered the door. As I turned to leave I pointed out to him that it was beginning to rain and his lawn mower was outside. "Thank you," he replied, "I'll get the grass cut in the morning – I'm retired."

"Good gracious, you look too young to be retired," I commented, and turned down the path. As I closed the gate he ran after me. "Too young to be retired!" he exclaimed. "I'll tell you how old I am, luv. It used to be the wife who went to bed with headaches. Now it's me."

The Rt Hon Kenneth Clarke MP

Member for Rushcliffe, Secretary of State for the Home Office

On a walkabout in Southampton with James Hill, who was standing for re-election, I was approached by a rather rough looking man, who knew me and who asked who the "other man" was. Taking a chance, I said, "This is your Member of Parliament, James Hill."

"He is no MP," said the man in what appeared to be a scornful voice. I held my breath as I wondered what was coming next.

"He is no MP," the scruffy man continued, "he is a GOD!"

Well! I thought, I wouldn't quite go that far!

"He is no MP," repeated the man, "he is a God, he got me transferred from a prison I didn't like to one that I did!"

The Rt Hon Peter Lilley MP

Member for St Albans, Secretary of State for Social Security

During the election, I was accompanying a candidate on a visit to a boot factory in his constituency. The time came for a "photo opportunity", and the managing director obligingly handed the candidate an enormous example of their produce to hold up in front of the cameras.

The candidate thought he would get tremendous headlines, along the lines: "Tory puts the boot in". But I warned him in the nick of time: "You can't let yourself be photographed like that. The headline will be all over the papers tomorrow: 'Tory given the boot.' "

He said: "Thank you, Peter. You saved me from putting my foot in it."

The Rt Hon John Biffen MP

Member for Shropshire North
(Leader of the House of Commons and Lord Privy Seal 1983-87)

I learned with resignation that Shropshire North was to receive a General Election visit from Edward Pearce, gifted satirical *Guardian* columnist and opera buff. Obviously the organisation and I had to be in tip-top form. Fate decreed otherwise. The celebrity visitor was directed to a non-existant village square, he was shoe-horned into an already over-loaded car, and he had to endure a senior north Shropshire Tory's assertion that the media (not just the opinion polls) should be closed down for the last ten days of an election campaign.

Worse was to follow. The highlight of the Pearce visit was to be a spell of canvassing in Lyneal, a hamlet more than half forgotten by time. Initially all went well. A highly competent retired army officer had organised an effective candidate's "blitz" on the village. It involved a visit to a potato farm where the technical discussion on potato marketing seemed to render our distinguished visitor comatose.

My wife and two stepchildren were part of our team visiting Lyneal. They, of course, are experienced campaigners but now under military guidance, they were told how to "recce", report back and assemble for departure. We were all given our plans, and "estimated time of arrival" for the next "blitz" – the nearby village of Welshampton.

So the team, in their several vehicles, left Lyneal taking on Edward Pearce, perhaps wiser on the potato issue than he had ever been. Welshampton was to provide coffee or sherry and a more general view of politics. Imagine the confusion, and recrimination – when it was discovered that my stepson Nicholas had been lost in the transfer.

The military efficiency of the Lyneal visit, the mastery of the potato problem, the impression of a well-organised campaign, all had been set at nought. If I could not look after a stepson, how on earth could I be trusted to look after a voter?

Fortunately the misery was short-lived. Nicholas realised he had been unwittingly abandoned and hitch-hiked to Welshampton, arriving in time to join us as we were deploring Neil Kinnock's qualities of leadership.

Our celebrated visitor just beamed. The organisational efficiency and political sophistication of north Shropshire were now in a proper context. Should Edward Pearce widen his talents beyond the *Guardian* to be a librettist? You can already see the title page, "The Lost Stepson".

Richard Wilkinson
Parliamentary Candidate for Kilmarnock and Loudoun, 1992

As in most constituencies at General Election time, our local secondary schools organised an "election hustings" featuring the four candidates – Conservative,

Labour, SNP and Liberal Democrat. Unfortunately, I could not attend the event due to a family bereavement, and yet in my absence I recorded ten votes in the ballot at the end of the meeting which I considered not bad given the nature of the constituency. Not on our winnable list, you know.

Next day, I did attend a similar "hustings" meeting with some of the other candidates at the local Technical College in front of three hundred students. After a brilliant exposition of Conservative Party policies and achievements by myself and miserable defeatist speeches from my opponents . . . the public spoke through the Ballot Box – Labour won by a short head in front of the SNP candidate with the Liberal Democrat not present. The Conservative? The Government candidate? Me? I got three votes (I actually only *saw* two but the MP assured me that I got another).

My conclusion is therefore that I get more votes by not turning up at meetings. Fortunately, at their age, not many had the real vote.

The Rt Hon the Lord Boyd-Carpenter

(MP for Kingston upon Thames 1945-72, Chief Secretary to The Treasury 1962-64)

A candidate at a public meeting got embroiled with a very determined heckler. The dialogue ended with the candidate saying, "You are very difficult," to which the reply was, "I know. We both are. But the difference is that I am trying to be and you cannot help it."

Nothing Whatsoever to do with the Election

John Watson

(MP for Skipton and Ripon, 1979-87)

I was invited to start the Burnsall Fun Run. I thought I might have to wave a handkerchief, fire a small starting gun or even just shout "go". So I was unprepared when an elderly local wing commander produced a huge pistol with a polished wooden handle and a flared barrel. It was loaded, he said. Treating the instrument with the utmost respect I pointed it straight up at a tree, told the runners to get on their marks and pulled the trigger.

Pandemonium. The bang was so loud that none of the runners started. The believed some terrible accident had occurred. After a moment's silence the air was filled with the crying of babies, the barking of dogs and the approach of a police vehicle.

But for me the silence continued. No one else had stood so close to the gun. As the commotion died down and the runners set off up the hill, shaking their heads, I wandered in a world of my own round the cake stalls, white elephant stalls and tombolas. All constituents, friendly and unfriendly, were greeted with the same bewildered smile.

Only gradually did my hearing return. It was finally restored 48 hours later during a speech by Ian Paisley!

Edwina Currie MP

Member for Derbyshire South
(Under-Secretary of State for Health, 1986-88)

I'm still collecting graffiti.
In a college in Warwickshire, not far from Stratford, someone had written:

Shakespeare was a transvestite!

And underneath:

I should know! signed Ann Hathaway (Mr).

Then there are the more virulent ones, of which my favourite was in Exeter:

Get Maggie before she gets . . . aagh . . . !

and under a poster in our local bus garage advertising a union meeting called to discuss strike action:

We have ways of making you walk.

Peter Thurnham MP

Member for Bolton North East

Consolidated Fund Debates are a series of short debates that run through the day and night, finishing at 8.30 in the morning. I had been drawn number 13 and it was thought that I might just get in before the debate finished, but it was unlikely that I'd come on before 6.30 am.

My flat is the near to the House of Commons, so I left a message with the attendant who sits at the back of the Speaker's Chair, to telephone me in good time before my debate was expected, should it come on rather early. I set my alarm for 5.50 am and went off to sleep.

About 1.30 in the morning, I heard the phone ring and my daughter answered it; unknown to me it was a nuisance caller who had been pestering my daughter, so she took the phone off the hook, not knowing that I was waiting for a call myself! At 5.50 am I telephoned the Whip's Office to see how the debate was going.

"Where have you been?" they said, "We have been trying to ring you. Someone has been round knocking on the door of your block of flats. You are needed immediately."

I had to dress at record speed and rush round to the House of Commons, getting into the chamber just in time to hear the Speaker call my name for a somewhat breathless contribution to the debate.

The Rt Hon the Lord Prentice

(MP for Daventry 1979-87, Minister for Social Security 1979-81)

Sometimes, events which seem important to us, and even to the media, make very little impact on our constituents.

In 1977 I crossed the floor of the Commons and joined the Conservative Party. There was a great deal of publicity.

A few months later an elderly cockney lady came to my advice bureau at East Ham Town Hall. She explained her housing problem and I promised that I would try to help.

As she was leaving she said firmly: "I've voted Labour all my life, so I expect you to help me now."

Patricia Rawlings MEP

Member for Essex South West

As an MEP I travel a great deal and occasionally to campaign with my colleagues for elections in other countries. Recently I was campaigning for the UDF in the Bulgarian General Election with a Spanish and an Irish colleague. During a meeting which was progressing very slowing I became, I'm afraid, a little impatient.

My Spanish colleague tried to soothe me by saying, "Relax! we have an expression in Spain which you may know. It's 'mañana'. We shall get there in the end."

Unsoothed and still fretting I asked the Irish colleague sitting next to me if they had a word for "mañana" in Ireland.

"Yes," he replied, "but it doesn't carry the same degree of urgency!"

Anthony Simpson MEP

Member for Northamptonshire and South Leicestershire

Euro-MPs as a race tend to spend a large part of their time away from home. One MEP had spent a week away in Strasbourg followed by a week in Brussels. He returned home exhausted on the Friday night, slumped into bed beside his wife and slept the sleep of the blessed.

At about three in the morning there was a terrific crash downstairs. He awoke, somewhat disorientated, sat bolt upright in bed and said: "My God, I think your husband's come home!" To which his wife murmured sleepily from the pillow. "Don't worry, darling, he's still in Brussels!"

Graham Smith
Constituency Finance Advisor, Conservative Central Office

I was Nigel Lawson's Agent at the time of his resignation from Government. He was clearly depressed when I saw him the day after it all happened and so I decided to try and cheer him up by asking him for some advice.

"Nigel," I said, "you know I was Leon's Agent and he resigned; now I'm with you and you've resigned. Who would you like me to go and work for next?"

His reply was not entirely audible!

The Rt Hon David Hunt MP
Member for Wirral West, Secretary of State for Wales

A funny thing happened to the elderly peer who dreamt that he was speaking in the House of Lords – and then woke up to find that he was.

Peter Thurnham MP
Member for Bolton North East

Eric Forth decided to make the public announcement about my appointment as his PPS when he came to speak to Bolton Business Ventures. Anxious to look by best for the photograph, I arranged for my hair to be cut by my secretary's daughter Julie. After Julie had washed my hair, she discovered that she had left all her scissors and other implements at a house where she had been to cut someone else's hair, so she had to dash out to get them.

She was away a long time and I began to fret about whether I'd be ready for Eric Forth when he arrived. Julie eventually got back, having had to buy a new set of implements because the person whose hair she had cut had gone out leaving the house locked. By the time she cut my hair it was too late for me to be photographed with Eric Forth in the presence of the Mayor. No one believed my excuse – I was late because the hairdresser had lost her scissors.

Russell Matthews

Agent, Wokingham Conservative Association

Having retired from the Services I became Sir William van Straubenzee's Agent. To be near at hand but just outside the constituency, my wife and I bought a house in Hampshire.

A week went by and a delightful, elderly, grey-haired lady, complete with a fat Jack Russell in support, knocked on my door.

After the usual pleasantries and some probing, she asked me if I was a Conservative. At this stage I was most impressed that my new village organised an efficient "road warden, welcome new residents' system". I confirmed that I was indeed a Conservative whereupon she asked me if I would join the local Association.

"No thank you," I replied.

"Why not?" indignantly.

"Well you see, I am William van Straubenzee's agent and consequently I am a member of the Wokingham Association," I explained.

"You're not one of THOSE are you? Come on Freddie we're wasting our time here." Turning on her heels, she departed.

Nineteen years have passed and I still live in the village but I have not met my "Conservative welcome lady" again.

Sir Dudley Smith MP
Member for Warwick and Leamington

As a representative of the British Parliament on the Council of Europe in Strasbourg for many years, I have heard all kinds of mistakes made by the interpreters who, I stress, achieve a generally high standard and are very conscientious. There is one particular gaffe which is remembered long after the event.

Some years ago, the "father" of the Irish Delegation, the late Mr Oliver Flannagan – a lovely man – waxed very indignant during an important debate on genetic engineering and the "brave new world" of scientifically planned children. Like most of his countrymen, he was never at a loss for words. A very prominent Roman Catholic, he espoused his religious cause with fervour.

In his oration he said: "And isn't it outrageous, if these plans go ahead, that we shall establish banks of frozen semen?" The French-speaking members of the Assembly looked very puzzled as, over their earphones, there came the translation: "Isn't it outrageous that there will be rows of very cold matelots?"

The Lord Plumb MEP

Member for The Cotswolds

A funny thing happened to me while sitting on the rails of the sheep pens in Brecon market. A local farmer poked me in the back with his stick and said, "I'm not agin this Single Market you keep on talking about as long as you don't hold it on a Thursday, to clash with Brecon"!

Peter Bottomley MP

Member for Eltham

I recently received a letter from a constituent concerned about sex change operations addressed:
"Dear Sir or Madam"!

John Watson

(MP for Skipton and Ripon, 1979-87)

My secretary sprained her back in February 1987. She was lifting our Complaints file at the time. Had she been lifting our Thank You file the problem would not have occurred.

In eight years as an MP, my Thank You file attracted just twelve entries – and five of those were from one constituent in Giggleswick who believed, in error, that I had been effective in ridding his home of a plague of masonry bees.

Postscript

Chris Chope, who was sadly defeated at Southampton and is now on "sabbatical leave" from the Commons, recently received a letter from his Conservative Association seeking renewal of his subscription.

The letter began brightly:

"Dear Chris, 1992 has been a splendid year for us so far . . .!

J.C

List of Contributors